Remembering YOUR SPIRITED ESSENCE

BRIAN ROSCOE

REMEMBERING YOUR SPIRITED ESSENCE
COPYRIGHT © 2021 BY BRIAN ROSCOE

All rights reserved. No part of this publication may be reproduced, distributed, or transmitted in any form or by any means, including photocopying, recording, or other electronic or mechanical methods, without the prior written permission of the author, except in the case of brief quotations embodied in critical reviews and certain other noncommercial uses permitted by copyright law.

The content of this book is for general informational purposes only. It is not meant to be used, nor should it be used, to diagnose or treat any medical condition or to replace the services of your physician or other healthcare provider. The advice and strategies contained in the book may not be suitable for all readers.

Neither the author, publisher, nor any of their employees or representatives guarantees the accuracy of information in this book or its usefulness to a particular reader, nor are they responsible for any damage or negative consequence that may result from any treatment, action taken, or inaction by any person reading or following the information in this book.

For permission requests or to contact the author, visit:
brianroscoeauthor.com

ISBN-13: 978-1-957348-06-3

PRINTED IN THE UNITED STATES OF AMERICA

Remembering YOUR SPIRITED ESSENCE

"We are constantly invited to be who we are."
—*Henry David Thoreau*

So often we're all looking for an explanation, a picture, or description of our authentic self, but that authentic self doesn't inhabit us the way we think. Its form is ineffable and uniquely evasive and unpredictable. It's embodied more through a presence within us, and there are no words for its description, only a sense, perhaps a feeling, that we can't quite describe. Our authentic self is one with the infinite combination of everything that we experience in this creation, and, in our humanness, we're here to remember the essence of it. We're here to reclaim the highest form of our being, to reconnect with our so easily forgotten essence-awareness, our presence in this world and, within that, ourselves.

A Prayer

I am made of pure essence. Divine breath rises through me and I am its channel, my path flooded with its purpose. I bow deeply in gratitude as all of life opens through me. As truth flowing through my life, I am raised up into my journey, I open to this gift, and I celebrate all that life offers.

Remembering YOUR SPIRITED ESSENCE

Soon enough, you will get very tired of chasing anything but yourself and your connection with God, and even that will become redundant, until one day,

you just are.

Have you ever noticed the amount of time and attention paid to thinking about the things we want to avoid verses the attention given to working on the qualities and ways of being we'd like to acquire in our lives? It's curious how we can be; fear having more power over our minds than our desire to become. That, on a conscious as well as subconscious level, we're quick to run away from our growth, our expansion—that we're often prepared to run from or sidestep our own unfolding and work of life.

Growth is never about what you wish to avoid. To grow in this life, our thinking needs to be directed at what we want to attain. And every time we choose growth, we pull ourselves back into our power; we move back into ourselves.

Like fear in the spotlight on the stage of our life, the difficulty of being human comes when we focus on negativity and on what we don't want. We create vast arrays of suffering within as we put our energy into resistance to what is, or we throw ourselves into the ideas of the mind we're actually trying to avoid. We can literally make ourselves sick doing this. In focusing on the undesirable versus desirable, we deplete ourselves.

We look at life as a survival game, often selecting the worst case scenario as our attention target, subconsciously making it our goal, believing that anything less is acceptable and enhances our chances of an acceptable life. So our life ends up becoming a series of protection mechanisms, helping us head off perceived threats and protecting us against feeling too vulnerable or too much disappointment. We make it a life less than it can be through paying more attention to fear than growth.

Our job, our real work here in this human form, is to reinforce the vitality of living, to embrace the gift of life. **We need to bring focus to what we want rather than attention to what we fear will happen.** This is an exercise in neurology, a workout of the mind, centered in love and driven by the heart. Repeatedly reinforcing an idea of the mind, no matter what it is, creates a neurology, a framework within us, to build on in life. What we focus on, whether it's productive or unproductive, is our choice, but it's our productive neurology that holds the power of our life.

> *"Only the truth of who you are,*
> *if realized, will set you free."*
> *-Eckhart Tolle*

Remembering YOUR SPIRITED ESSENCE

Self-essence is in knowing, an awareness that always lays beyond the inquisitive fingers of the intellect; it's a knowing of oneself as a radiance, a heart, and far more than simply a physical body with a mind.

> There is an *awakening*
> that happens *within*
> as soon as you acknowledge
> the depth of your own self-essence.

When we come to a place where we can find an understanding that our existence and our reality comes before the intellect of the mind and lays far beyond where the mind can go, our heart suddenly becomes available to us in a way that engulfs our presence in this world.

Sometimes we forget why we're really here. It has little to do with accumulating those look-how-wonderful-I-am affirmation moments, or attending success building seminars, building up the bank accounts, or checking off all the resorts we've visited. Your purpose does not require you to look a certain way or have a particular living arrangement. This life was meant to first be a precious journey of growth. It's about being part of and connected to the deeper miracle of the life we're in, knowing the essence of our soul and learning how to bring that forward.

That's the stuff you don't need an affirmation for. That's a way of being that you can sit back with and simply be present to—no fancy clothes necessary… or at all! All our ego-centered desire need not be present. Pampering the insecure mind affirmation and praise are simply the ego's distraction. It's unnecessary to being in your life and inevitably weakens your journey, even though your mind tells you it makes you stronger.

So do the journey a favor: free yourself from the desire to be a particular way, the need to preform perfectly, or to be seen well by those who are too busy with themselves to even notice, and simply pay attention to the life that exists within, ready to unfold into the world from the core of your heart.

What intrigues us
in this life is the
*draw of our
own heart.*

The continuous pull of our truth. The understanding of love's presence within. The search for what's authentic within our being. The draw of the heart keeps us motivated and captivated with this journey of ours. It keeps us trying over and over again to *get life right*, and that opens us up to look at our mistakes and acknowledge our faults that keep us from stagnating in our minds. It's the draw of the heart that keeps us walking towards the truth of what's so very real inside of us.

It's the passions that we discover through our lives that most remind us of our own hearts. When we purely participate in that which we are passionate about, no matter what it is, it reminds us of the presence of love within. It's here that we participate in our life as hearts. We participate as we are meant to be: touching, playing the strings of the heart, being people in love. It might be simply by watching and adoring children at play, or doing art. It could be the passion of walking in the woods and being aware of the pure beauty of it all, or through the channeling of the creative heart in writing, wherever that takes us.

So, whether it's working on cars, social work in the community, prayer, church, school or learning of any kind, what we have a passion for is but a reminder of our ability to know love. A reminder of who we are and what we are meant to be. So embrace your passion. Its purpose expands within you.

*"Love, in its essence, is spiritual fire.
And we are the same, because we are love."*
—*Seneca*

The *whole*
of what we're here to do
is to allow our *human* form
to again meet our *spirit*.

Life presents vast and indispensable opportunity. It's an art and a journey to perfect our ability to fuse our physical walking world with the spirited essence of who we are.

Remembering YOUR SPIRITED ESSENCE

JOURNEY PROMPT

What behaviors, habits, addictions, or rigid ways of being that keep you distanced from your truth are you ready to give back to the universe, ready to free yourself from? They're qualities of being that you've acquired and held as your identity, albeit a false identity that really isn't you. These are the thoughts and actions that keep you in tension, stuck in judgment and ego, unhappy and in struggle. They are the ways of being that stunt your ability to move from a mere survival and fear-based dance of life and towards your more sacred dance of living through your heart—a dance where you're in your joy and can breathe knowing that you are an integral part of this miracle. *So, what do you need to let go of so you can release into who you truly are?*

We look at a newborn child with such jaw-dropping awe, and we giggle, become enchanted, gawk and swoon, commenting on how amazing, how infinite, how incredibly beautiful and inspiring they are. Amazed, we stand confronted by the awesome power of the creation of life. It's a wonderful feeling. But when do we stop doing that? When do we stop looking at one another, ourselves, our children, our old folks with that same awe that came so naturally when we found ourselves looking and giggling at that sleeping newborn child?

It seems like a sin against all creation to not see the brilliance of what we all are, and a sin against yourself not to see the brilliance and awesomeness of you. We get so caught up in our heads that we think we know something more than God (because God knows how amazingly brilliant we are), and we think God is wrong and we are not amazing, and we take ourselves and everyone around us for granted, missing the miracle in the miracle in the miracle that we are. We get lost, we forget who we are, and this is where evil begins; this is what makes sin possible.

JOURNEY PROMPT

List your top three to five inspiring moments or times when you were left with an ineffable feeling about your world. Have you ever thought about how that opened up your heart?

This journey of the spirit requires us to roll up our sleeves and immerse ourselves in the hard work of remembering—*remembering a deeper and ancient part of our spirited selves, remembering a more profound love implanted at the origin of our hearts, and remembering a life lived through our truth; a truth already held within.*

We all share a common origin and, equally, just through our human creation, we've been taken away from our purely spirited home. Here, our existence automatically becomes transformed into a journey that asks us to refine the art of stepping back into our truth. We're asked to search for and find an essence of life that we somehow lost connection with as we became spirit-fed humans. We've somehow forgotten in this world how to know our deepest truth. So, we spend our lives recovering ourselves, negotiating a voyage back to our long-ago forgotten spirit—an adventure faint in our minds and so difficult to recognize we can barely hear the quiet whisper of its origin.

But this remembering of our truth, constantly trying to reconnect with our origin, is the journey of life. Our work and struggles towards this end are not solitary attempts. We repeatedly approach the vague memories held within our hearts, hoping to remember a love and a life that can only be realized when our human form embraces our spirited identity.

There's no map for us to follow, and the journey's hard, but the destination is simple. It requires that you explore and manifest all the qualities of love you can muster. And all the work and maintenance… well, that's up to us.

"The strange paradox
is that when you
*accept yourself
completely,*
then you change."
–Carl Rogers

Remembering YOUR SPIRITED ESSENCE

JOURNEY PROMPT

Boots on the ground: who are you and how will you live your life?

Identify and list four qualities of what it is to feel strong and true. These are the qualities that you would always want to walk with through life.

"Hard times arouse an instinctive desire for authenticity."
-Coco Chanel

Opening to our truth, basically waking up to being alive, requires us to avoid hitting our oh-so-tempting awareness snooze button. It asks us to be awake to life, and to present ourselves to a deep way of being that refuses to put its head in the sand when resistance or discomfort shows up in any way in our world. We're asked to open ourselves with grace to that place within that begs us to let life begin!

Just like love, our awakening to truth, which is the truth of who we are, only needs permission to stay awake. Its declaration is: don't sleep through life, be in life, Know—Your—Truth!

JOURNEY PROMPT

Can you think of any situation that you feel like you want to hide from, but if you didn't a deeper self-knowledge, perhaps inner strength, might have a chance to evolve forward through?

- What might not hiding look like?
- How would that feel?
- Who might you become in that courageous effort?

No matter what story we come to believe defines us, no matter what thought we may be stuck in, when clinging to any idea or story about ourselves, we run the risk of losing touch with that deeper core awareness—our spirited identity.

Simply put, we exist, awakened within a body, and in this nanosecond, we are mysteriously and miraculously alive. Whatever ideas and personal dramas may be spinning through our minds, releasing them enables us to set aside our acquired belief systems, dogmas, and the burdened ways that don't serve our being present to the flow of life. Letting go opens us to hearing the quiet whisper of awareness, the blossoming within of what is so miraculous *and, in that, our aliveness becomes shockingly noticeable, all by itself.*

JOURNEY PROMPT

Can you see how easy it is to define yourself through your job, accomplishments, acquisitions, and relationships? And can you see that these things are only what you've done and where your interests lay, but not who you are? Which leaves you with the question: okay, then who am I? To which I shake your hand and say, "Welcome to the journey."

Remembering Your Spirited Essence

"The authentic self is soul made visible."
-Sarah Ban Breathnach

We're masters at covering up our truth, only to position ourselves to learn how to uncover it again. Welcome to the journey. Over and over again, we fall towards fear and then fight to rediscover our love and, in that, we reclaim life.

Our internal spark is the reflection of life itself and, ironically, it's our spark that we're all yearning to remember. But it was there before your conception, there at the moment you were born, it's always been, and you have always known its whisper.

When love seems far away and hard to find, life will ask us to reconnect with the truth of who we are, to remember our very obvious nature that we, indeed, are love.

JOURNEY PROMPT
Claim Life!

What does it look like when you walk in your truth, walk forward in love? How does that feel, and what happens to you when you do it?

Not living your *Truth* potentially infects all other aspects of your life.

JOURNEY PROMPT

Have you ever considered that swimming in polluted waters potentially pollutes anything in those waters? The same is true for the mind, so it's best to clean things up before inviting new thoughts to go for a swim. Throw a little compassion, your best integrity, and some understanding into that filter!

Connection with our truth, our love, the very core of what we are, is infinitely and permanently placed within our soul. This truth needs no help to evolve. Its sole requirement for growth is based in our persistent elimination of interference (distorted thought), around our awareness of and interaction with its presence. In this, we can see and know the true preciousness of who we are and what we were made to be.

IT'S THERE. You don't need anyone to find it for you. You simply need to recognize the truth of this life and step forward with deep attention toward the presence of the love that you are.

"If you want to reach a state of bliss, then go beyond your ego and the internal dialogue. Make a decision to relinquish the need to control, the need to be approved, and the need to judge. Those are the three things the ego is doing all the time. It's very important to be aware of them every time they come up."

-Deepak Chopra

Sometimes I sit back and think of the long list of things I fool myself into believing—all the stories I attach to in order to feel in control or important. I consider the "need" for the physical comfort, the ideas and assumptions of what personal relationships "should" look like. I look at all the churches, organizations, industries, and governments that want us to buy into their particular way of thinking, the politics, the news, and all the gossip of the world that begs for our attention. They ask for our blind belief in their particular slant of "reality," *their* promise for *our* journey. These groups of society ask for our belief in their ability to bring us happiness and peace.

But when we get caught up in outside beliefs, we end up forgetting who we are, we forget to honor our own personal truth, and we tune out our heart. Sometimes, we even enthusiastically give up our personal journey to follow someone else's truth, or their lies, but in our quiet moments, we do relent, we admit to the misery we feel and remind ourselves that this life is not based in what we receive from the outside. It's an inside job. This is the understanding that saves us, and as Rumi said, we remember our own great truth "beyond the worlds of right and wrong."

JOURNEY PROMPT

Losing yourself can happen slowly and insidiously, but sooner or later, it happens to everyone, and we suddenly we find ourselves with a confused look saying, "Hey! Where did I go?" wondering who we are, and unsure of just exactly what we've become. And then, in a lucid moment of thought, we catch a glimpse of our precious identity, and regardless of what's going on with our outside world, we see that this life is, indeed, our miracle to present ourselves into. And we do our very best to step forward and begin again.

THE MORAL: No matter what's rocking through your world, whether it's a tiny issue or a life-shifting drama, we will absolutely, always, always, always have the opportunity to begin again placed in front of us. It's our choice, and we get as many tries as we need.

FIND OUT FOR YOURSELF!

The Buddha said,
"Don't believe what I say. Find out for yourself."

This adventure of being a spirited human being is a journey of a very personal, profound, and curiously precious nature. It's a journey the universe is constantly begging us to partake in, putting us in a position to learn, to grow, and to remember ourselves, but we have to choose to take it. We need to embrace the opportunity. That's the job. We all have to *choose* to be free again.

The very essence of being alive asks us to take the driver's seat in our life. We're in charge of navigating all the turns, dead ends, U-turns, and detours. Continuously challenged to move forward, we're tasked with rediscovering our truest self. So, put a little gas in the tank, use the good high-octane stuff, and spin those new tires!

JOURNEY PROMPT

When we create rigid boundaries in our world, we inherently limit our access to certain, often unknown, possibilities of love's presence in our lives. Where are you so rigid that you limit what you can experience with others or what they can experience with you?

Remembering YOUR SPIRITED ESSENCE

> *"Your time is limited,*
> *so don't waste it living someone else's life.*
> *Don't be trapped by dogma, which is living with*
> *the results of other people's thinking. Don't let*
> *the noise of other's opinions drown out your own*
> *inner voice. And most important, have the courage*
> *to follow your heart and intuition. They somehow*
> *already know what you truly want to become.*
> *Everything else is secondary."*
> *-Steve Jobs*

It's not easy being put here as a *spirit* trying to be a form.

Addicted to and stuck in our physical form, we live our lives continuously being distracted away from living and moving through our hearts. To get ourselves back to that place of authentic expression takes work, persistence, and a quality of thought that cultivates true personal strength and a very real opening to the love that we are.

Over and over again, you have a chance to be in your life, to be present to a light that honors your endowed gift of being a spirit with a body. We need to step up to the gift! Be present in to the ride and embrace it! Own it! Love it in a way that says, "Oh my god, this life is so precious despite any perceived shortcomings. However this happened, however I got here, thank you. I will honor this."

"If the only prayer you ever say in your entire life is, 'Thank you,' it will be enough."
-Meister Eckhart

JOURNEY PROMPT

If you had no body, no needs of the body (yes, including sex AND voyeurism), if you couldn't feel hungry, if you had no ego attachment to news or current issues, if you simply existed as a product of your spirit in your own authentically true nature, what might that look like? What would you do with your time? What kind of energy would you want to bring into the world? How well would you love?

THIS IS ACTUALLY A VERY BIG QUESTION. Give yourself some time to dwell on it for a bit. When you have a sense of what this might be like, then give yourself a body. Keep all those other distractions (yes, like sex) out of your way for the moment. How might you see and approach people? Can you see how you might be able to look at everyone differently, without judgement or fear? Can you imagine how you might approach them differently, more purely? You might want to try and hold onto that.

Christians, Muslims, Buddhists, atheists—everyone, in the deepest part of their heart, only desires to know their truth. Sometimes, followers get caught up in their desire to make sure everyone else sees "truth" the same way; often in a way that doesn't reflect anything but their dogmatic belief systems—systems that bring no peace. This renders their hearts and the hearts of those who buy into their beliefs impotent in spirit. It is, and always will be, impossible to know the truth in the depth of your heart as long as you are attached to the idea that you know and others don't. The very idea of that indicates an arrogance and a disconnection from the gentleness of spirit that comes with knowing God, knowing the truth of oneself. How do I know this? I don't.

JOURNEY PROMPT

Think of any of the inflexible opinions, judgments, or belief systems you hold (you're human, we all got 'em!). These are the concepts you hold dear, at least in your judgmental reptilian mind, that help keep you feeling safe, separate, or feeling really "special."

Example: Do you love chocolate ice cream and feel repulsed by those who enjoy vanilla bacon ice cream? Do you have compassion for the poor and resent the top 1%? Do you question the authenticity or moral values of vegans, vegetarians, hunters, meat-eaters, drinkers, smokers, drivers of certain cars, or people who dress a certain way? Well, welcome to your judgment! It all boils down to this: We are all individuals, and if we want to find peace, we need to learn to love our differences instead of judging them. Liking is optional, loving is mandatory.

"The spirituality of our time is the awakening of the consciousness of humanity to the divinity in the heart of every person."
-Hazrat Inayat Khan

Life is a long series of working through our struggles and our joys, and experiencing the healing that comes through them. It's these very struggles and joys that act as the catalysts of life—these are the events that root us into our journey, handing off their message and positioning us on the path toward whatever the next adventure of life and healing is meant to be, emotionally, physically, or spiritually.

Consciously, we don't always know the best path to take, and this probably works to our advantage. It keeps our judgmental mind out of the way, but over and over again we're resetting ourselves to grow, we're asked by a relentless universe to become ourselves again, to move towards something closer to our hearts. And our healing doesn't always come all at once—it tends to be incremental, and although it may not always be clear what's going on, healing and life itself simply require the presence of our peace, our trust, and our attention and faith in our own growth. We're only asked to do our best in any particular moment of the experience.

JOURNEY PROMPT

It sure seems like an endless evolutionary process of exploring what it is to be human, and maybe it is endless, but every time you reset toward your next level of healing and growth and reorient yourself toward your next step in life, that's also the step that sets you up, yet again, for your next step forward, movement toward the next something more in your journey to yourself. Yes, it's an endless spiral of the spirited human experience, which is apparently… infinite. So, be open to and embrace the infinite journey of you! It unfolds in untold, always surprising, and unexpected ways.

BECOMING
[INSERT YOUR NAME HERE]

Being on this journey requires us to participate in continuous acts of self-love. It asks us to remember our truth and to open up to becoming what we're meant to be. It's fruitless to try and copy anybody else's journey; pointless to try and mirror their traits with the intention of succeeding for yourself. It doesn't happen that way. Observing the ways of others only serves to generate question marks and points of interest for us to meditate on. Ultimately, we have to find ourselves through ourselves; find a way to make all the qualities that touch our hearts ours. Becoming ourselves is a matter of remembering what truth and beauty already

Remembering YOUR SPIRITED ESSENCE

exists within us, and becoming who we are in our individual, authentic, only-ours-to-be way. Welcome to your life. Welcome to becoming [insert your name here].

JOURNEY PROMPT

These are questions worthy of exploration, questions that prompt transformation. Be patient with yourself as you try to find words you use to describe yourself, words that help you understand your journey. Sometimes the language for it comes slowly, so take your time as they evolve within your heart. Allow your ideas, your words, your understanding to flow, not so much from your head, but through your open heart, and take note!

- When you can let go of the outside influences that distract you from being you, what is that like?

- What does it feel like to allow yourself to stand in your strength, free from any desire to belong to anyone or anything but yourself? Who are you in that space?

- Who do you become when you stand alone and free? Who is that magnificent being?

- How does it look, what does it feel like, and who do you become when you claim your freedom and *own who you are*?

- What is life like when you're not controlled by the desire to have things in any particular way, free from your quest to attain something outside of yourself to "complete" yourself?

- Who are you when you free yourself to be free in yourself?

Our journey asks for nothing less of us than our entirety. Our commitment is one of maintaining the path back into ourselves; one of completely actualizing love's full presence within.

Remembering YOUR SPIRITED ESSENCE

This life of ours is big, and we have so many reasons and excuses to step back from our truth. It takes dedication to our journey if we want to reconnect with that deep love that's true to our identity.

Be **persistent** and **consistent**,
while maintaining your attention
on your *intention*.

"We are made to persist.
That's how we find out
who we are."
-Tobias Wolff

OPENING TO THE GIFT

Howard Thurman says,
"Don't ask yourself what the world needs; ask yourself what makes you come alive, and then go and do that. Because what the world needs is people who have come alive."

In our quiet moments, we find ourselves desiring something more of this life, not knowing exactly what it looks like, but we know it exists and that we'll know it when we see it.

We suspect we're missing the bullseye, that there's more to the journey than what we've been given—a root reality that exists beyond words that asks us to keep stepping forward toward our insatiable desire to know better, and through that, to find our way to act better. This is our awakening—our calling to explore our hope, our truth, and ourselves. This is us opening to the gift.

As soon as you see that you're stuck in the way of your journey, it's a kind of victory for you, a kind of recognition of having been off track that automatically means you're back on track... until, of course, you're off track again!

Around it goes, and where it stops, nobody knows.

So, welcome to your own personal never-ending and fantastic journey of being human. All you can do is learn how to love the ride.

"As a single footstep will not make a path on the earth, so a single thought will not make a pathway in the mind. To make a deep physical path, we walk again and again. To make a deep mental path, we must think over and over the kind of thoughts we wish to dominate our lives."
-Henry David Thoreau

The fusion between the matter and spirit of life always seeks its highest expression in this world, which, ironically, is one of us finding our way back to our true nature.

Above all, be present to your love, be yourself, and don't let anything pull you away from that gift—not fame or fortune, friends or family. Your truth is the first and only possession given to you, and no one can take your essence away.

Remembering YOUR SPIRITED ESSENCE

You can believe that you've given yourself away, lost your truth, but essence is the one thing that will always be accessible; the miracle that when asked for, will always reflect you back to your brilliance.

Don't mistake your need to become more in this world with apathy about who you already are.

JOURNEY PROMPT

Our personal truth is a gift to be held precious. Even though our self awareness and our individual identity may appear to change over time, when we walk through life with the intention of creating more love, we're only becoming more of who we are, remembering more of our ancient truth. Sometimes we choose a path that's expedient, and sometimes one that seems relentlessly slow and requires far more patience. But smile, because as an old saying goes, "The oxen may be slow, but the earth is patient."

Remembering YOUR SPIRITED ESSENCE

We're all put here on this earth, challenged to find ourselves, all on the journey of searching for, finding, and knowing our value here. It's a journey that's required of us, and we're asked to learn how to embrace it without question. To know that we belong in this world in a full, deep, and loving way. There's a hugeness, an unexpected and vast sense of personal acceptance and love associated with it. When we can connect to our self-love as a gift that we give ourselves, subsequently, it becomes a beautiful gift we give to one another, and in presenting our gift to everyone we touch, we accept it in an even more complete way for ourselves.

It's not so much that we need to *wake up*, because *our True nature* is awake! Our challenge is one of not sleeping through the experience of *being alive.*

www.ingramcontent.com/pod-product-compliance
Lightning Source LLC
Chambersburg PA
CBHW021432070526
44577CB00001B/176